EXOPLANETS

Sally Ride
Science

EXOPLANETS

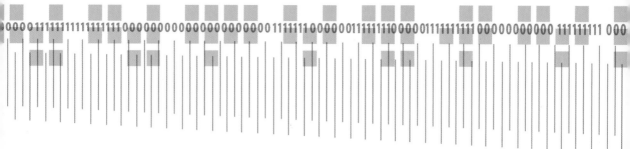

CONTENTS

EARTH, ONE PLANET AMONG MANY

Are we alone? In our solar system, yes! None of the other seven planets that travel around our Sun have intelligent life. What about primitive life? We don't know. There may be microbes on Mars. There may be primitive life way out in the underground oceans on Jupiter's moons. But certainly nothing you could carry on a conversation with.

other suns out there—many, many, many, just like our own. And orbiting some of those stars are other planets. How many? No one knows.

We're just starting to learn about those other planets. They are a long way from our solar system. Most aren't very much like Earth. Since discovering the first of those planets in 1995, we are getting better at it. We find more and more of them each year, including smaller and smaller worlds closer in size to Earth. It may be just a matter of time before we discover one that is just like our home planet, Earth.

So maybe we're not alone after all.

Some of the world's most powerful telescopes sit above the clouds on top of Mauna Kea, the highest mountain in Hawaii. They are helping us search for planets around stars beyond our solar system.

raph by Jean-Charles Cuillandre (CFHT), © 1998.

MILKY WAY GALAXY

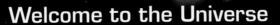

Welcome to the Universe

Look up on a clear, dark night and sometimes you can see a fuzzy band of light—the Milky Way galaxy—stretching across the sky. We live in this galaxy. Our solar system is nestled in one of its spiral arms.

What lies beyond our little neighborhood in space? A Universe so immense it's mind-boggling. The amazing photo in the background on these pages takes us deep into the Universe and shows us thousands of galaxies. But, unbelievably, the photo still shows only a tiny, tiny speck of the sky you can see. Welcome to the Universe!

SOLAR SYSTEM

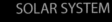

EARTH

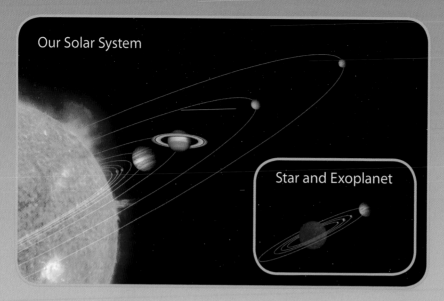

Our Solar System

Star and Exoplanet

Inside *v.* Exo

Astronomers call the planets around other stars "exoplanets" since they are found outside our solar system. *Exo* is Latin for "outside." Think of *exo*planets as being found *outside* our little neighborhood, the solar system.

In Your Lifetime . . .

We have a long history of exploring other planets—at least in our solar system. People have gazed at the planets around our star, the Sun, for thousands of years, studied them through telescopes for hundreds of years, and sent spacecraft to explore them for dozens of years. But planets around *other* stars? It wasn't until 1995 that astronomers even discovered the first one. Now, after just a few years, they have found more than 200 of these exoplanets. Each month, the number grows—with no end in sight.

Three hundred and fifty years ago, Isaac Newton could barely see into our solar system using his small telescope (left). Today, astronomers can peer deep into space using powerful telescopes like the Spitzer Space Telescope (above). The SUV-size Spitzer has spied exoplanets around distant stars.

What Took So Long?

Astronomers have been scanning the sky for centuries. Why did it take them so long to find even one exoplanet? Because planets are much smaller and much, much dimmer than stars, so they're very, very hard to see. Why are they dimmer? Stars generate huge amounts of energy at their centers. When that energy makes its way to the star's surface, it's released as light. Planets don't generate their own light. They just reflect some of the light of a star nearby. So exoplanets stayed hidden until we came up with clever ways to detect them and new technology that made detection possible.

Stars shine but planets only reflect light. The planet Jupiter is the brightest object in this scene. That's because it's much closer to us than any of the stars. Whose light does Jupiter reflect?

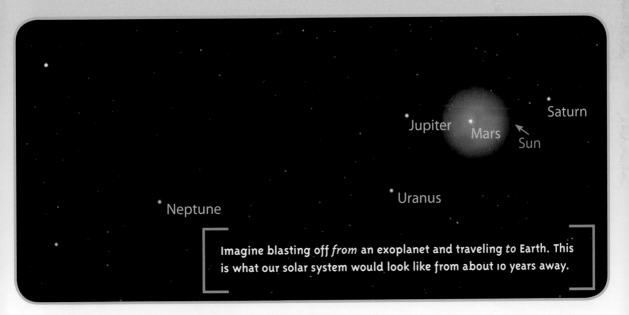

Imagine blasting off *from* an exoplanet and traveling *to* Earth. This is what our solar system would look like from about 10 years away.

Yoo-Hoo, We're Over Here!

It's been a huge discovery to learn that there are other planets out there. Maybe there *is* one just like Earth. Maybe its inhabitants are looking for us!

IT ALL FITS IN THE UNIVERSE

The Universe contains all of space—including every galaxy, star, and planet. It was born in a tremendous explosion called the Big Bang 13.7 billion years ago. It's been expanding ever since.

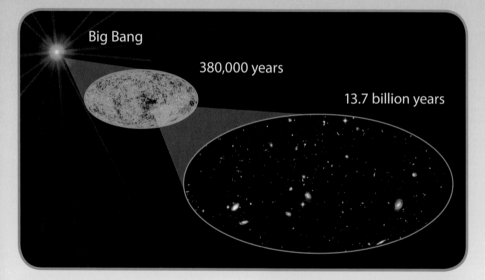

Big Bang

380,000 years

13.7 billion years

Billions and Billions . . .

The Universe is home to billions and billions of galaxies. And each galaxy is home to billions and billions of stars. Where do we fit in? We're nestled in a spiral arm of the Milky Way galaxy—along with 100,000,000,000 (that's 100 billion!) other stars. When it comes to stars, don't think our Sun's the only one.

Our Sun

From Earth, the Milky Way looks like a shimmering path of white. That's just the sideways view. Here's what it would look like "from above."

Run for Your Calculator

How many is 100 billion? If you began counting now, it would take you 3,000 years to count that high. Better get started!

4 U 2 Do

Penny-Stepping

What does a billion look like? Suppose you started in Los Angeles, California, with one billion pennies (that's 10 million dollars in pennies!) and started laying them side by side. By the time you laid them all down, how far would you have walked? Where would you be? (Hint: the diameter of a penny is about 20 millimeters, or 2 centimeters.)

Check out your answers on page 38.

Medium Isn't Small

We call the star at the center of our solar system the Sun. But it's really just a star, like billions of others. Our Sun is a type of star called a G2. That means it's a medium–sized yellow star. But don't think medium is anywhere near small—our Sun's diameter is 110 times that of Earth's.

> Do you get a warm feeling looking at this picture? You should. It's our Sun—our very own star.

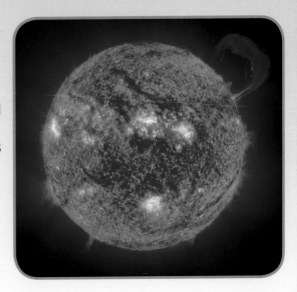

Only Five Billion to Go

Old mister Sun is almost five billion years old. Nothing lasts forever, but don't worry about the Sun blinking out anytime soon. Yellow stars like our Sun last about 10 billion years, so it's only middle-aged!

All in the Family

A star and the planets that circle it form what is called a solar system. *Sol* is the Latin word for "sun," so *solar* means anything having to do with a sun. Our solar system is made up of our Sun and its planets—Mercury, Venus, Earth, Mars, Jupiter, Saturn, Uranus, and Neptune. It also includes the dwarf planets Pluto, Ceres, and Eris, and busloads of comets and asteroids.

Our Not-So-Limited View

For now, the search for exoplanets is limited to nearby stars—just those in a small corner of the Milky Way. Why? Because they're really hard to see! Even our most powerful telescopes can find planets only around the closest stars. But if you're looking for other planets, that's still a lot of places to look.

The Milky Way has more than 100 billion stars, so there are hundreds of millions of them "near" us.

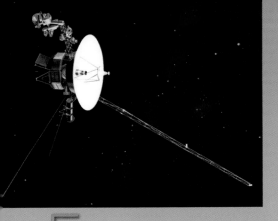

Not-So-Instant Message

Other stars are so distant that astronomers use light-years to measure how far away they are. Some of the closest exoplanets orbit a star called Gliese 876, but they're still about 15 light-years away. If you pointed a powerful flashlight at Gliese today, the light wouldn't get there for 15 years! Who knew "close" could be so far?

The *Voyager 1* spacecraft is farther from Earth than any human-made object. It's 100 times more distant from our Sun than Earth is. Still, it won't come near another star for thousands and thousands of years, even traveling at 39,000 mph!

Universal Speed Limit

A light-year is the distance that a beam of light can travel in a year. Light moves faster than anything else in the Universe. In a way, you can think of the speed of light—about 300,000 kilometers (186,000 miles) a second (yes, a second!)—as the speed limit of the Universe.

Mega-Journey

The Milky Way is about 100,000 light-years across. That's huge! Most of the exoplanets found so far are much closer to home—just a couple of hundred light-years away. Still, even the zippiest spacecraft would take tens of thousands of years to reach them.

4 U 2 Do

Pack an Extra Bag

Another nearby solar system is around the star Epsilon Andromedae. It's 10.3 light-years from Earth. Any light from its star has taken more than a decade to travel to your eye. If you think that's a long time, calculate how long it would take to travel just a single light-year—9,500,000,000,000 kilometers (5,900,000,000,000 miles)—using the following vehicles. Remember, a typical year is 8,760 hours long.

Car (95 kilometers per hour/60 miles per hour)

Jet aircraft (950 kph/600 mph)

Voyager 1 spacecraft (63,000 kph/39,000 mph)

Check out your answers on page 38.

HOW WORLDS COME TOGETHER

Headed for Hollywood?

Interstellar space—the space between the stars—is full of huge clouds of gas and dust. Sometimes one of those clouds begins to contract. As it collapses, it flattens out to form a spinning disk. Think of pizza dough spinning in the air. Then the gas and dust at the center collapse even more, and become so dense and so hot that . . . a star is born! And it has a very bright future.

Demolition Derby

What about the stuff left in the spinning disk? It begins to clump together. The clumps collide and grow to the size of a grapefruit, then an SUV, then a mountain. Eventually, some get big enough to pull themselves into balls and clear out the smaller chunks of rock in their paths. These biggest survivors are planets—still whirling around the new star. Earth formed in this way, and scientists think the process is common. So lots of stars should have planets around them—the clumps that survived the early demolition derby.

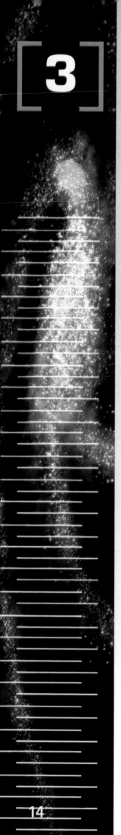

Just the Beginning

Until a few years ago, we didn't even know if planets existed around other stars. Today, astronomers know of several hundred in our corner of our galaxy alone. The easiest exoplanets to find are those much, much bigger than Earth that orbit very, very close to their stars.

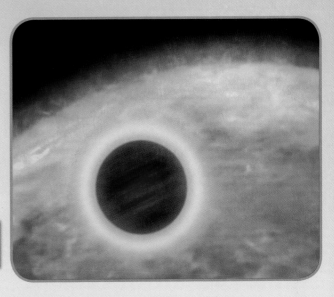

Exoplanet HD 209458 b

Big and Gassy

Most of the exoplanets astronomers have found so far are huge balls of gas—something like Jupiter and Saturn. Jupiter's the largest planet in our solar system. You could fit more than 1,300 Earths inside it. But Jupiter is only about 320 times more massive than Earth. That's because Jupiter's made mostly of the two lightest gases—hydrogen and helium—so it's much less dense than our rocky Earth.

Earth

Jupiter

HD 209458 b

4 U 2 Do

Exo-Sized

Jupiter's diameter is 11 times bigger than Earth's. In turn, the giant exoplanet HD 209458 b has a diameter that is 1.3 times bigger than Jupiter's. If Earth's diameter is about 12,756 kilometers (7,296 miles), what is Jupiter's diameter? How about HD 209458 b's diameter?

Check out your answers on page 38.

Dense Makes Sense

Some planets are denser than others. Size has nothing to do with it—remember Jupiter compared to Earth? Complete this list of pairs of similar items (they might both be fruits, kinds of rocks, and so on). Fill in each blank with a similar item that is either denser or less dense than the item given. We did the first one for you.

LESS DENSE	DENSER
Ping-Pong ball	Softball
_____	Bowling ball
_____	Salt water
Angel food cake	_____
Metamorphic rock	_____
_____	Coconut
Styrofoam peanut	_____

Check out your answers on page 38.

Big and Easy

Since astronomers have found only a few hundred exoplanets, it's too early to say what's typical. Just because astronomers have found lots of huge planets, doesn't mean they're the most common. It's just that they have been the easiest to find!

This drawing shows one view of the Neptune-size exoplanet, 55 Cancri e, circling its star, 55 Cancri.

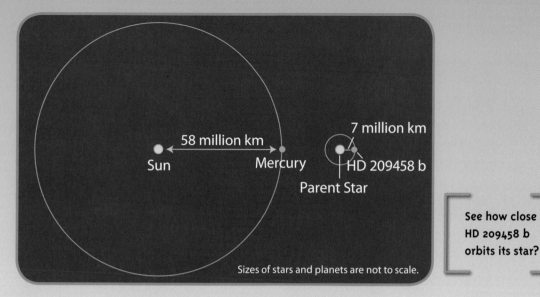

58 million km
Sun
Mercury
7 million km
HD 209458 b
Parent Star
Sizes of stars and planets are not to scale.

See how close
HD 209458 b
orbits its star?

Where a Week Could Be a Year

Most of the exoplanets found so far orbit really close to their parent stars. It takes Earth 365 days to go around the Sun—that's our year. Mercury, the closest planet to our Sun, whirls around it in only 88 days. But some exoplanets are so close to their parent stars that they whip around in just a few days. That would make for a short school year!

Only Their Names Are Boring

The planets in our solar system are named for figures from ancient mythology, like Mercury, Venus, and Mars. Exoplanets don't have such interesting names. Astronomers name them for the stars they orbit. For example, Gliese 876 b is a planet that orbits the star Gliese 876. The first planet found around a star is called "b." Astronomers know of at least three planets around Gliese 876, so they are called Gliese 876 b, c, and d. What happened to "a"?

Sunrise, Sunset, Sunrise, Sunset . . .

Imagine what it would be like to explore an exoplanet. Some exoplanets have two—count 'em, two!—suns instead of just one. That's a lot of sunrises and sunsets. How would you divide night and day?

What would it be like to stand on the surface of an exoplanet's moon? This drawing puts you on a rocky moon looking up at a real exoplanet, HD 188753 Ab, that orbits three suns. How's that for a pretty *suns-set*?

Debra Fischer

Astronomer
San Francisco State University

So who's finding these exoplanets? Meet Debra Fischer. "My job is to go to work and find worlds around nearby stars," Debra says. Each year, Debra makes regular visits to telescopes in California, Hawaii, and Chile to look for those planets. She spies on 50 to 150 stars a night. Finding exoplanets has become almost routine. But routine doesn't mean boring. Her team keeps discovering more and more weird worlds and oddball solar systems. "Anything is possible," Debra says. While big planets are easier to find, it's becoming clear that planets like our own are probably much more common. They may even orbit all stars. "It's possible they all have rocky planets. We're just the rocky debris left over from star formation." She and a small group of other astronomers have worked together to find more than half of the exoplanets that we know. "These tiny little steps we've taken in the last decade to find other planets are just the beginning," she says.

Being There

Hot or Not?

Some exoplanets whirl around their suns in wild and wacky orbits—nothing like the nearly circular orbits of the planets in our solar system. When a planet is much closer to its sun during one part of the orbit than during another, what effect might that have on the planet?

Out of This World

You can't blame astronomers for assuming that exoplanets would be a lot like the planets we know in our solar system. But as they discover more and more of them, they're learning that just about anything is possible. These are some wacky worlds out there.

Tails, You Lose

Heat can make planets do some crazy things. One exoplanet is gradually losing its atmosphere because its sun is boiling it away. The escaping gas gives the planet a giant, cometlike tail.

HD 209458 b

Whirlwind World

This planet has scorching hot temperatures all the time, even though half of it lies in permanent darkness. Astronomers think super-high winds sweep the planet, constantly moving heat around in its atmosphere and keeping things toasty everywhere.

HD 179949 b

Ice Place to Visit

There are a handful of "super Earths" that weigh anywhere from 5 to 15 times as much as our world. These are huge ice balls that quickly froze together around cool, small stars called red dwarfs.

OGLE-05-169L b and possible moon

Darkness at Noon

The atmosphere of one exoplanet is chock-full of tiny grains of dust. Dust is really good at blocking light. Astronomers think the planet is completely hidden by the dust, making it one of the darkest worlds we know.

HD 189733 b

Moon? Planet? Moonet?

The big star (far left) is 55 Cancri with its family of exoplanets. Planets may even form around failed stars called brown dwarfs (upper right). Brown dwarfs are no bigger than some exoplanets, so astronomers think they really should be called moons. Others disagree. What do you think?

Two exo-versions of solar systems

[It can be easy to find Mars at night.
Just look for the reddish planet.]

Stars in Their Eyes

When you look up in the night sky, you can see Venus, Mars, Jupiter, and Saturn. With a small telescope, you can find Uranus and Neptune. Mars looks bright at night, but that's nothing compared to the brightness of the Sun. You never see Mars during the day because the Sun is way too bright.

2 Close 2 See

Some astronomers say looking for an exoplanet is like trying to spot a firefly next to a faraway lighthouse at night. The distant planet is like the firefly—hard to see because the star it orbits is so much larger and brighter than it is.

Aha!

Exoplanets are just too far away and too faint to see directly, even through the strongest telescopes. So how do astronomers find them? These intrepid planet detectives stake out the stars, looking for clues that they might have something orbiting around them.

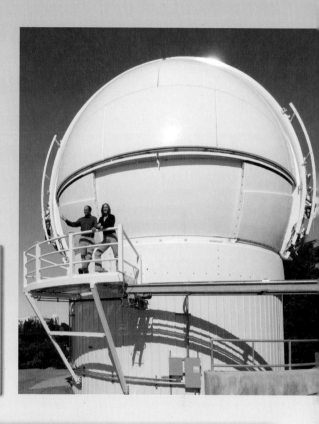

Planet detectives Geoffrey Marcy and Debra Fischer stand on the catwalk of the almost-completed dome of the Automated Planet Finder Telescope. They watch the same stars over and over every night for months before they can learn if there are any exoplanets circling them.

4 U 2 Do

Friendly Planet

Let's explore what happens to the Sun's light when a planet zips in front of it. Set up a lamp on a table in the middle of a dark room and have a friend slowly walk circles around it as you watch from the side. Pretend the lamp is a star and your friend is an orbiting planet. Does the lamplight dim each time your friend passes between you and the lamp? Congratulations! You've just detected a "planet."

Something's Come Between Us

Astronomers can also "see" exoplanets when they get in the way of their stars. Whenever a planet passes in front of its star, it blocks some (though very, very little) of its light. That means the star will dim just a tiny bit. With modern, sensitive instruments, astronomers can watch the star's light get slightly fainter every time the planet circles in front of it. Since bigger planets block more light, they're easier to find this way than smaller planets are. Down in front!

Star

Exoplanet

Don't Twinkle, Little Star

Some of the largest telescopes on Earth are being used to hunt for new planets. But moisture, dust, pollution, and heat in Earth's atmosphere can distort the view from the ground. They make it look as though a star "twinkles." Not a problem in space. Space telescopes are letting astronomers find planets that are smaller and farther away. Twinkly little stars? Good for poets, but bad for astronomers.

An artist's drawing of the Spitzer Space Telescope and a distant Earth. Spitzer needs to stay cool to watch for the infrared light—heat—of stars and other objects in space. Part of the telescope is kept chilly inside a space "thermos."

Eye in the Sky

The Hubble Space Telescope (below) can detect a star dimming when a Jupiter-sized planet passes in front of it. Astronomers have used its observations to estimate that there may be six billion planets that size in the Milky Way. That's six *billion*! And that's just in our little galaxy.

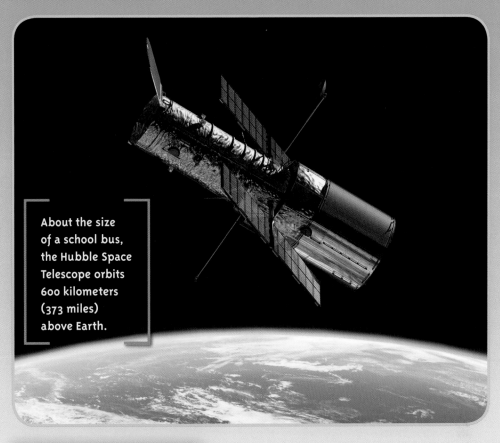

About the size of a school bus, the Hubble Space Telescope orbits 600 kilometers (373 miles) above Earth.

How Do They Know?

Tug and Wobble

All planets tug on their parent stars and make them wobble. How powerful is that tug? It depends on the size of the planet. The bigger the planet, the stronger its gravitational pull on its star. The big ones tug harder and make their stars wobble back and forth more than smaller planets do. Astronomers watch a star over many months to see if it wobbles in regular ways. If it does, it's probably because of the gravity of an unseen planet hiding nearby.

Exoplanet Nursery

While it orbits around Earth above our atmosphere, the Spitzer telescope is also studying exoplanets. It investigates the swirling disks of dust and gas around stars. Those disks are where planets form. So it's peeking in on the formative years of newborn exoplanets.

Coming Up Dry . . . Then Wet

The Spitzer telescope also got the first "sniff" of the atmosphere of an exoplanet. The results caught scientists by surprise. They thought it would detect water vapor in the gases of the alien world. Instead, the atmosphere was as dry as a bone. Later, other scientists found evidence of water around another exoplanet, HD 209458 b, using observations from the Hubble Space Telescope. Imagine detecting water in the air of a planet 150 light-years from Earth!

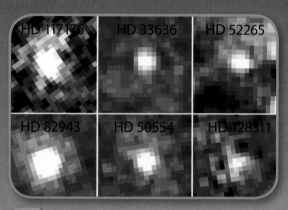

The yellow fuzzy blobs are stars circled by disks of dust and some exoplanets.

World Vision

You can't see exoplanets with your naked eye or a backyard telescope, but some of the stars they orbit are parts of well-known constellations you can find in the night sky. Some of the most recognizable constellations—Andromeda, Cancer, Gemini—have planets around them. What's your favorite constellation? Have planets been discovered around any of its stars?

When a Star Blinks . . .

Scientists can estimate the mass of a planet—how much stuff it's made of—by measuring how it tugs on its star and makes it wobble. They can estimate its size by measuring how much light it blocks when it moves in front of its star. Once they know both the size and the mass of a planet, astronomers can calculate its density. Density tells them a lot about what a planet is made of—would it float in a tub of water (like Saturn), or sink like a rock (like Earth)?

Experts Tell Us

Charles Beichman

Astronomer
California Institute of Technology

The search for exoplanets is a modern job that only a couple of hundred scientists around the world do. Ask an astronomer, like Charles "Chas" Beichman, when this work began, and he'll tell you 2,500 years ago. The basic questions we wonder about—like "Where did life come from?" and "Are we alone?"—are the same that used to puzzle ancient Greek philosophers, Chas says. "What makes today different than the past is, today we can use science to answer those questions," he explains. Chas is helping to move more of the hunt for exoplanets into space, where in the next few decades powerful telescopes will speed up the search. But don't think it'll be over any time soon, he says. "This is going to be a 50-year voyage of discovery—and it's just starting."

THE HUNT FOR WORLDS LIKE EARTH

Astronomers are finding bunches of big exoplanets. And the more they look, and the better their instruments get, the more they find. Now astronomers are starting to find planets more like Earth. As telescopes and detectors get better and better, they'll be able to spot more of the smaller planets. Perhaps planets just about our size— rocky worlds, with conditions that might support life.

Goldilocks and the Habitable Zone

When Goldilocks tasted the three bowls of porridge, one was too hot, one was too cold, and one was just right. The same is true of planets—some are too hot and some are too cold, for life. Astronomers are beginning to find the first ones that may be "just right." In our own solar system, Venus is too hot, and beyond Mars it's too cold. But, lucky for us, Earth is "just right." Earth is in what's called the "habitable zone" of our solar system. Goldilocks might say it's where life could *bear* to live.

Ah . . . Just Right

What makes the "habitable zone" habitable—a place where living things could exist? It's the part of the solar system where it's possible for water to exist on a planet's surface. Too near the Sun, all the water evaporates. Too far from the Sun, it all freezes. In between, the temperature's just right—and that's where you could find water. What's so special about water? Water is one of the ingredients that's needed for life to take hold and thrive.

Exo-Life?

On Earth, life began in water. And scientists believe water is absolutely necessary for life. So they are looking for planets about the size of Earth, and in orbits sort of like Earth's. Finding another rocky planet like ours that's a comfortable distance from its star would mean it could have water on its surface. And that would mean it could have life, too.

Small Is Big

Astronomers cheered when they first spotted a new planet circling the star Gliese 581. The new planet, Gleise 581 c, is small—only five times heavier than Earth and possibly a rocky world. They nicknamed it Goldilocks because it orbits inside the habitable zone—where life could exist. Gleise 581 c is 14 times closer to its sun than we are to ours. In our solar system, that would make things scorching hot. But its sun is so dim that astronomers thought the planet might be cool enough for water to exist. Their hopes were dashed when it was discovered that the planet is actually sizzling hot—way too hot for life. So the planet hunters continue the hunt.

An artist's drawing of Gliese 581 c circling a dim star in the constellation Libra.

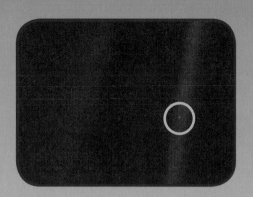

Blue? Wah-hoo!

Astronomer Carl Sagan called Earth a "pale blue dot" because that's just what it looked like in a photograph taken by the *Voyager 1* spacecraft when it was 6.4 billion kilometers (4 billion miles) from home. Astronomers hope to find another blue dot, rich in water and oxygen, around another star someday.

Being There

Alien Report: "It's Earth!"

Suppose you were an alien astronomer and it was your spacecraft, not *Voyager 1,* which took that photo of Earth. Would you see clues that our planet was special? Yes! You would know it's a small, rocky planet in the habitable zone of its solar system. Your instruments would detect clouds of water vapor in its atmosphere, indicating it probably had liquid water on its surface. Call a press conference!

Breath of Fresh Air

As an alien astronomer, you would also find strong hints that Earth has life. That's because you'd find oxygen in Earth's atmosphere. Why is that an important clue? Oxygen combines easily with other gases, so it doesn't last long in an atmosphere. So if an atmosphere is rich in oxygen, something on the planet is constantly replenishing it. That "something" is probably life!

When seen from space, the Earth's atmosphere is thin. Without it, we would have little protection from the harshness of space.

Thanks for the Air

On Earth, oxygen is made through photosynthesis. That's when plants use energy in sunlight to turn carbon dioxide and water into food. As part of this process, plants release oxygen into the air or water. They "breathe" it out, so we can breathe it in.

Aquatic plants release oxygen into the water. See the bubbles?

How Do They Know?

Two Big Clues

Space telescopes are beginning to study the gases that make up the atmospheres of exoplanets. Depending on what they find, astronomers can make educated guesses about whether a planet is home to life. Finding two gases—water and oxygen—would strongly suggest life is present. But these exo-sleuths won't be able to solve the real whodunit—Is the planet home to simple life, like bacteria, or something more complex?

Who's On the Job?

In the future, a spacecraft called *Kepler* (left) will be able to keep watch on 100,000 different stars. It will look out for exoplanets that are similar to Earth. Another set of spacecraft, called *Terrestrial Planet Finder*, will have instruments that will enable them to measure the size, temperature, and orbits of small, Earth-like planets—and even study their atmospheres to look for gases that suggest the presence of life.

IS ANYBODY OUT THERE?

Can You Hear Me Now?

While some scientists are looking for planets that could support life, others are skipping ahead and looking for direct evidence of intelligent life. Off and on for almost 50 years, scientists have listened for radio signals from outer space that could have been sent by alien civilizations. Is anybody out there? So far, no signal. But scientists are still listening, so who knows?

ET—Phone Us

The hunt for signals from ETs—*extraterrestrials*—uses special telescopes called radio telescopes. They don't collect light, like the telescopes you look through. Radio telescopes collect radio waves, which also travel at the speed of light. When you turn on your radio, you're listening to music that traveled through the air at the speed of light to your radio's antenna. Scientists think that advanced alien civilizations might send messages out into the Universe to let other civilizations know they're out there. Better tune in.

Director
Center for SETI Research

Jill Tarter has always wondered about other worlds, and the life that might call those places home. When Jill was a little girl, she used to visit relatives in Florida where she and her dad would take walks on the beach at night and gaze at the stars. "It always seemed natural to me to assume those stars were someone else's sun," Jill says. Today, Jill runs a project that isn't looking for other worlds—she and other scientists have jumped ahead and have begun looking for laser flashes and listening for radio signals from aliens on those planets. "One of the motives for the search for exoplanets is to find a place where ET might live. We leapfrog over that. It might be possible to detect ET's technology without ever knowing the planet is there," Jill says. The SETI project is building a telescope that, when finished, should be able to scan 40 billion stars at the center of the Milky Way. The project has already checked out most of the stars known to have planets. No, it hasn't heard anything yet. SETI is tuned in. Is ET?

How do you "listen" for radio waves? With giant "ears," of course! Your house could fit inside this huge radio dish (left).

Reruns on the Run—and, Oh, Is Anyone Looking for Us?

Do we send signals out to space? You bet—every day. Radio and television signals that are broadcast through the air also travel out into space. Those signals travel at the speed of light toward the stars. That means some of the first TV broadcasts are now more than 50 light-years from Earth. Aliens could be watching old reruns of "I Love Lucy" right now.

The television programs someone watched on this antique TV already are tens of light-years away from Earth.

That's One Long Conversation

Even if we detected an alien signal, we couldn't visit whoever sent it. The planet would be way too far away—so far away that we couldn't have much of a conversation, either. Signals from an alien world would take years and years to travel to Earth. And our reply would take just as long. Imagine communicating with a planet ten light-years away. It would take ten years to ask, "How are you?" and then another ten years to get an answer back. You'd be a senior citizen by the time you exchanged a few sentences. So, scientists plan a more one-sided conversation. We'd do lots of listening and learning.

From high atop the summit of Mauna Kea in Hawaii, astronomers hunt for exoplanets with the twin Keck Telescopes.

Your Turn

Not long ago we didn't even know if planets existed around any star besides our Sun. Today, we know of more than 200. And this is just the beginning. As we gaze deeper into space, we learn about the countless stars out ther and the planets that orbit them. Each year we discover new exoplanets, always looking for a planet that might be like Earth. Your generation will take over the search. What will you discover?

OUR PATH TO
EXOPLANETS

Since ancient times, people have gazed at the stars in wonder. Their imaginations created patterns and stories out of groups of stars. These are called constellations. Look, there's Ursa Major, the great bear. There's Draco, the dragon. Astronomers today are filled with the same sense of wonder, but they have powerful telescopes to peer deeper into space. These hi-tech tools have helped astronomers uncover some of the biggest mysteries of the Universe—including the amazing recent discoveries of exoplanets orbiting stars beyond our solar system.

200

1995
The very first exoplanet is discovered. It orbits the star 51 Pegasi in the constellation Pegasus. It's 51 Pegasi b.

PEGASUS

2004
55 Cancri e is found—the fourth exoplanet circling the star 55 Cancri.

CANCER

1996
55 Cancri b is found—the first of four exoplanets found orbiting the star 55 Cancri.

1995

1996

1997

1998

1999

200

URSA MAJOR

1996
Astronomers spot 47 Ursae Majoris b. Then they discover the first of three exoplanets orbiting the star Upsilon Andromedae in the constellation Andromeda.

1999
Two more exoplanets are found orbiting Upsilon Andromedae.

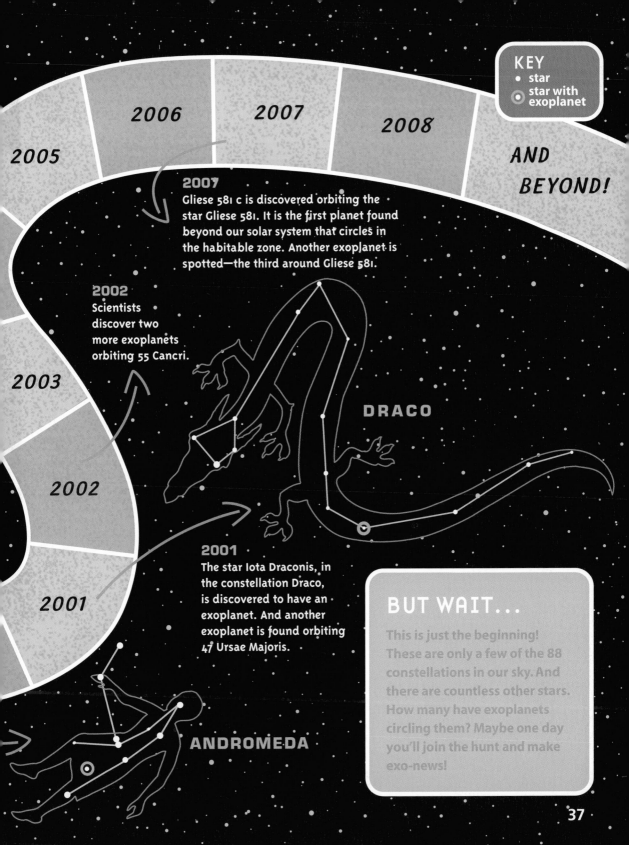

KEY
- star
- ⊙ star with exoplanet

2007
Gliese 581 c is discovered orbiting the star Gliese 581. It is the first planet found beyond our solar system that circles in the habitable zone. Another exoplanet is spotted—the third around Gliese 581.

2002
Scientists discover two more exoplanets orbiting 55 Cancri.

2003

2002

2001

DRACO

2001
The star Iota Draconis, in the constellation Draco, is discovered to have an exoplanet. And another exoplanet is found orbiting 47 Ursae Majoris.

ANDROMEDA

BUT WAIT...

This is just the beginning! These are only a few of the 88 constellations in our sky. And there are countless other stars. How many have exoplanets circling them? Maybe one day you'll join the hunt and make exo-news!

37

asteroid (n.) Small rocky object that orbits the Sun. Thousands of asteroids orbit in a region called the Asteroid Belt, which lies between the orbits of Mars and Jupiter. However, some have been found in other orbits, including some that cross Earth's orbit. (p. 12)

astronomer (n.) A scientist who studies celestial bodies, including planets, stars, galaxies, and other astronomical objects. (p. 8, 9, 13, 15)

comet (n.) A small body made up mainly of ice and dust, in an elliptical orbit around the Sun. As it comes close to the Sun, some of its material is vaporized to form a gaseous head and extended tail. (p. 12)

constellation (n.) A group of stars that appears to form a recognizable shape in the sky. (p. 26)

dwarf planet (n.) A celestial body that orbits a star, is big enough that its gravity has pulled it into a round shape, but has not cleared its path of other objects. (p. 12)

exoplanets (n.) Planets that orbit stars other than our Sun. (p. 8, 9, 13, 15, 16, 18, 20)

galaxy (n.) A large collection of stars bound together by gravity. Our Sun is one of billions of stars in the Milky Way galaxy. (p. 7, 10)

gravity (n.) The attractive force that any object with mass has on all other objects with mass. The greater the mass of the object, the stronger its gravitational pull. (p. 24)

interstellar space (n.) The space between stars in a galaxy. (p. 14)

light-year (n.) The distance that light travels through space in one year. Light moves at a speed of about 300,000 kilometers (186,000 miles) per second, so it travels about 10 trillion kilometers (6 trillion miles) in one year. (p. 13, 34)

Milky Way galaxy (n.) Our own galaxy. It has a spiral shape, and our Sun is one of its billions of stars. (p. 7, 10, 13, 25, 33)

orbit (n.) The path of one body around another, as a result of the force of gravity between them. Examples are a planet's path around the Sun or a moon's path around a planet. (p. 5)

planet (n.) In our solar system, one of the eight major bodies that orbit the Sun. More generally, a celestial body that orbits a star, has cleared its path of other objects, and is big enough that its gravity has pulled it into a spherical shape. (p. 4, 5, 8, 9)

radio telescope (n.) Large instrument used to detect radiation from space at radio wavelengths. (p. 32)

solar system (n.) The Sun and all the bodies that orbit it, including Mercury, Venus, Earth, Mars, Jupiter, Saturn, Uranus, and Neptune and their moons; the dwarf planets, Pluto, Ceres, and Eris and their moons; asteroids; and comets. (p. 4, 5, 7, 8, 11, 12)

star (n.) A glowing ball of gas held together by its own gravity and powered by nuclear fusion in its core. (p. 5, 8, 9, 10, 11, 12, 13)

telescope (n.) An instrument used to collect and focus light to produce a magnified image of a faraway object. (p. 8, 12, 19, 23, 24)

Answers

4 U 2 Do, page 11
19,999 kilometers (12,427 miles)

4 U 2 Do, page 13
Car—11,225,266 years
Jet aircraft—1,122,526 years
Voyager 1—17,270 years

4 U 2 Do, page 15
Jupiter—140,316 kilometers (87,188 miles)
HD 209458 b—1,824,108 kilometers (1,133,448 miles)

IMAGE CREDITS
NASA/JPL/Caltech: cover, bookplate, p.17, p. 18, p. 21 bottom, p. 24. Jean-Charles Cuillandre (CFHT): pp. 4-5. NASA, ESA, S. Beckwith (STScI) and the HUDF Team: pp. 6-7 background. The International Astronomical Union/Martin Kornmesser: p. 7 middle. NASA/GSFC: p. 7 bottom, p. 12 bottom. NASA/JPL/Caltech/T. Pyle (SSC): p. 8 top. The Royal Society: p. 8 bottom. Vivian L. Hoette/Reproduced with permission from the Hands-On Universe project, Lawrence Hall of Science, University of California, Berkeley and Yerkes Observatory: p. 9 top. NASA/JPL: p. 8 middle, p. 9 bottom, p. 12 top, p. 13 top, p. 14 bottom, p. 16 bottom, p. 29 bottom. NASA/WMAP Science Team: p.10 top. NASA/JPL/Caltech/R.Hurt (SSC): p. 10 bottom, p. 20 bottom. Byron Hardy: p. 11 top. Trish Parisy: p. 11 middle. SOHO: p. 11 bottom. NASA/LaRC; p. 13 bottom. NSC/Robert Gendler: p. 14 top. NASA, ESA, and G. Bacon (STScI); p. 15 top. Roman Podgórny: p. 16 inset top. Robert Horvath: p. 16 inset bottom. Laurie Hatch: p. 19, p. 23. Hubble ESA Information Centre: p. 20 top. David A. Aguilar (CfA): p. 21 top and middle. Chris Schur: p. 22. National Park Service: p. 23 top. Karen Hom: p. 23 bottom. European Space Agency: p. 25. NASA/JPL/Caltech/C. Beichman: p. 26 top. Jerry Lodriguss: p. 26 bottom. Jim Keller: p. 27. NASA: p. 28, p. 30, p.32. USDA/Scott Bauer: p. 29 top. Bill Harada: p. 31 top. NASA Ames Research Center: p. 31 bottom. Seth Shostak, SETI Institute: p.33. Shaun Lowe: p. 34 top. Isaac Gary: p. 34 bottom. Courtesy W. M. Keck Observatory: p. 35.